AMAZING
BUILDINGS

FIRST EDITION

Project Editors Anna Lofthouse and Caryn Jenner; **Series Editor** Deborah Lock;
Senior Art Editor Cheryl Telfer; **Project Art Editor** Jacqueline Gooden;
Art Editor Nicky Liddiard; **US Editor** Elizabeth Hester; **DTP Designer** Almudena Díaz;
Pre-Production Producer Nadine King; **Producer** Sara Hu; **Jacket Designer** Chris Drew;
Indexer Lynn Bresler; **Reading Consultant** Linda Gambrell, PhD

THIS EDITION

Editorial Management by Oriel Square
Produced for DK by WonderLab Group LLC
Jennifer Emmett, Erica Green, Kate Hale, *Founders*

Editors Grace Hill Smith, Libby Romero, Michaela Weglinski;
Photography Editors Kelley Miller, Annette Kiesow, Nicole di Mella; **Managing Editor** Rachel Houghton;
Designers Project Design Company; **Researcher** Michelle Harris; **Copy Editor** Lori Merritt;
Indexer Connie Binder; **Proofreader** Larry Shea; **Reading Specialist** Dr. Jennifer Albro;
Curriculum Specialist Elaine Larson

Published in the United States by DK Publishing
1745 Broadway, 20th Floor, New York, NY 10019
Copyright © 2023 Dorling Kindersley Limited
DK, a Division of Penguin Random House LLC
22 23 24 25 26 10 9 8 7 6 5 4 3 2 1
001-333881-May/2023

A catalog record for this book
is available from the Library of Congress.
HC ISBN: 978-0-7440-7144-3
PB ISBN: 978-0-7440-7145-0

DK books are available at special discounts when purchased in bulk for sales promotions, premiums,
fundraising, or educational use. For details, contact: DK Publishing Special Markets,
1745 Broadway, 20th Floor, New York, NY 10019
SpecialSales@dk.com

Printed and bound in China

The publisher would like to thank the following for their kind permission to reproduce their images:
a=above; c=center; b=below; l=left; r=right; t=top; b/g=background

Alamy Stock Photo: imageBROKER / Jochen Tack 19br, REUTERS / Mark Baker 24-25t; **Bridgeman Images:** Look and Learn 11t;
Dreamstime.com: Lyda Feoli 16bl, Johnson175 26tr, Klodien 23cr, Steve Mann 27cr, Mistervlad 14-15t, Melinda Nagy 18,
Plotnikov 23tl, Shutterfree / R. Gino Santa Maria 12bc; **Getty Images:** De Agostini / DEA / G. DAGLI ORTI 14br;
Getty Images / iStock: nfensom 26-27

Cover images: *Front and Spine:* **Dreamstime.com:** Jenifoto406

All other images © Dorling Kindersley
For more information see: www.dkimages.com

For the curious

www.dk.com

AMAZING BUILDINGS

Kate Hayden

Contents

Buildings Around the World

A big city like this has all kinds of buildings. There are tall buildings, wide buildings, office buildings, apartment buildings.

There are weird and wonderful buildings all over the world. They are built to be both useful and fun to look at.

Pyramids

The pyramids in Egypt were built over 4,000 years ago. These monuments were made as burial sites for Egyptian kings and queens and their treasure.

To build the pyramids, workers had to drag heavy stones up a ramp, one by one. The pyramids were built to last for a long time.

Many Hands
It took 4,000 people 20 years to build the biggest pyramid.

The Colosseum

The ancient Romans built a massive amphitheater called the Colosseum. The Romans were the first to use concrete to make buildings.

The Colosseum was oval-shaped
and seated up to 50,000 people.
The Romans loved to watch trained
fighters, called
gladiators,
battle each other.
Cheers and boos
from the crowd
made echoes
all around
the stadium.

Castle

This fairy-tale castle, perched on a craggy hilltop in Germany, is called Neuschwanstein (NOY-shvan-stine). Earlier castles were built to protect the people inside, who could spy on approaching enemies from the tall towers. But this castle was built just to look beautiful.

A Disney Castle

Does this German castle look familiar? Cinderella's castle in Disneyland is modeled after this castle.

Palace

One of the world's biggest palaces is at Versailles (ver-SY) in France. It has over 2,000 windows, 1,200 fireplaces, and 67 staircases.

Fit for a King
The King's bedroom was at the center of the palace. Louis XIV even signed papers in bed!

There is also a Hall of Mirrors at Versailles. When the palace was built over 300 years ago, mirrors were very rare. Visitors were amazed to see their reflections.

The Eiffel Tower

The Eiffel Tower in Paris, France, is made of iron. It was the tallest building in the world when it was built. It took two years, two months, and five days to build.

In those days it was unusual to make buildings out of metal. Since then, metal has been used to make buildings taller and taller.

Extra Strength
The criss-cross pattern of the metal bars gives the Eiffel Tower extra strength and stability.

Skyscrapers

The tallest buildings of all are called skyscrapers because they seem to touch the sky.

The Burj Khalifa in Dubai, UAE, was the world's tallest skyscraper in 2010. It stands at 2,716 feet and six inches (828 m) tall. The giant building has 163 floors. Visitors can take in views from observation decks on the 124th, 125th, or 148th floors.

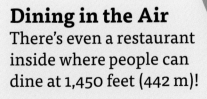

Dining in the Air
There's even a restaurant inside where people can dine at 1,450 feet (442 m)!

Spaceship Earth

Have you ever seen a building in the shape of a ball?

The round building in this picture is called Spaceship Earth. It's at the Epcot theme park at Walt Disney World in Florida, USA. Over 11,000 triangles cover the surface to make it look perfectly round.

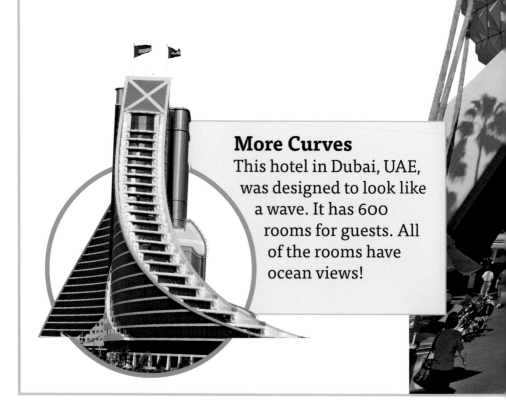

More Curves
This hotel in Dubai, UAE, was designed to look like a wave. It has 600 rooms for guests. All of the rooms have ocean views!

More Modern Buildings

Think of the amazing shapes
of other modern buildings.
What do these buildings
look like to you?

The Sydney Opera
House in Australia
looks like the
billowing sails
of a sailing boat.

The Guggenheim Museum in Spain may remind you of a large ship.

A Gleaming Roof
The roof of the Sydney Opera House is covered by over one million ceramic tiles.

Stadiums

Look at this huge stadium. Stadium Australia was built for the games of the 2000 Olympics. It was designed to be friendly to the environment. This means it uses less electricity for lights and air conditioning.

Olympics
New stadiums are often built for special events, such as the Olympic Games.

The stadium has big tanks to collect rainwater that falls on the roof.
The rainwater is recycled to water the field and even to flush the toilets!

The Eden Project

Where can you grow
bananas indoors?
In a giant greenhouse!
At the Eden Project
in England, the latest
technology is used
to create habitats
from around the world.

Even when it's cold and dry outside, the weather is hot and damp inside the Humid Tropics Biome.

Jungle plants grow as if they are in the middle of a rainforest.

The International Space Station

One of the most amazing modern buildings is way out in space.

All of the parts needed for the International Space Station are delivered there from Earth by spacecraft. Who knows what other amazing buildings may be built in the future?

Glossary

Amphitheater
[amp-fuh-THEE-ter]
An open-air building in an oval
or circular shape with raised rows
of seats

Gladiators
[GLAD-ee-ators]
Professional fighters who lived
in ancient Rome

Greenhouse
A closed structure—usually made
of glass—that is kept warm
and humid to care for plants
throughout the year

Palace
A large building that serves as the
official home of the leader of a
country or government

Skyscrapers
A very tall building that
generally has more than 40
or 50 stories inside

Spacecraft
Vehicles used to bring people
and cargo between Earth and
outer space

Stadium
A very large building, usually
without a roof, with tiers of seats
for people to sit and watch
sporting or entertainment events

Index

Quiz

Answer the questions to see what you have learned. Check your answers in the key below.

1. How many people did it take to build the biggest pyramid in Egypt?

2. What kind of building is the Colosseum?

3. What is one of the world's biggest palaces and where is it located?

4. What was the type of material and pattern used to build the Eiffel Tower?

5. What is the weather like inside the Humid Tropics Biome at the Eden Project in England?

1. 4,000 people 2. An amphitheater 3. Versailles, located in France
4. Metal bars in a criss-cross pattern 5. Hot and damp